60 Easy Piano Pieces

Compiled and edited by
John Ross

Access to Online Audio
https://esmistudio.com/pianobook.zip

Copyright © 2024 John Ross
Copyright © Miller Publications

ISBN: **978-176-3795600**

CONTENTS

1 Traditional and folk melodies

2 Greensleeves (*English Traditional*)
3 The Bells (*English Christmas Carol*)
4 We wish you a merry Christmas (*England, XVI century*)
5 Oh Susanna (*Traditional*)
6 Chiapanecas (*Mexican folk song*)
8 Deep River (*Spiritual*)
9 A haunted story (*unknown author*)
10 For He's a Jolly Good Fellow (*English folk song*)
11 Frankie and Johnnie (*Traditional*)
12 He's got the whole world in his hands (*Spiritual*)
14 Hornpipe (*unknown composer*)
16 Jericho (*unknown composer*)
17 Korobeiniki (*Tetris Theme*)
18 Kum ba yah! (*Spiritual*)
19 Loch Lomond (*Scottish folk song*)
20 On Top of old Smoky (*traditional*)
21 Petrushka (*Russian folk song*)
22 Roman Holiday (*unknown composer*)
23 Standing in the Need of Prayer (*Spiritual*)
24 Steal Away (*Spiritual*)
26 Tumbalalaika (*Yiddish Folk Song*)
27 Waterloo Hornpipe (*from Scotland*)

28 Classical music

29 Bourlesq (*from music book for Wolfgang*)
30 Menuet (*W.A.Mozart*)
31 Menuet Christian *Gottlob Neefe*)
32 Menuet (*Leopold Mozart*)
33 Allemande (*Joseph Haydn*)
34 O sole mio (*E. di Capua*)
36 Swabian Dance (*Leopold Mozart*)
37 Joy to the World (*G.H Händel*)
38 Can-Can (*J.Offenbach*)
39 Menuet (*J.S.Bach*)-
40 Für Elise (*Ludwig van Beethoven*)
41 La Donna e Mobile (*Giuseppe Verdi*)
42 Menuet in C (*Leopold Mozart*)
43 Shall we gather at the River (*Robert Lowry*)
44 Trumpet Tune (*Jeremiah Clarke*)
45 Walz in A Moll (*Frédéric Chopin*)

47 Jazz and blues

48 Got the Blues (*unknown composer*)
49 Got those Blues! (*unknown composer*)
50 Rock it away! (*unknown composer*)
51 Baby Elephant Walk (*Henry Mancini*)
52 Boogie-Woogie Goose (*Willard A. Palmer*)

53 Classy Rag
54 Fascination (*Filippo Marchetti*)
56 In the Mood (*Joe Garland*)
58 Jazz-Ostinato in Cis-Moll (*unknown author*)
60 Kiss the Rain (*Yiruma*)
62 Light and Blue (*Willard A. Palmer*)
63 Mamma Mia (*ABBA*)
65 Over The Rainbow (*Harold Arlen*)
66 River flows in you (*Yiruma*)
70 Septakkord-Swing (*unknown author*)
71 Sing the Blues (*unknown composer*)
72 Why am I blue? (*unknown author*)
73 Singin' in the Rain (*Nacio Herb Brown*)
75 Variations of a Shanty (*Willard A. Palmer*)

76 Music from films

77 Africa (Toto) (*D.Paich/J.Porcaro*)
78 Entry of the Gladiators (*Julius Fučík*)
80 Forrest Gump - Main Title (*Alan Silvestri*)
83 Moon River (*Henry Mancini*)
85 The Pink Panther Theme (*Henry Mancini*)

Traditional and folk melodies

Part I

Greensleeves

English traditional

The Bells

English Christmas Carol

♩ = 100

The bells in the stee-ple are ring-ing to-day!
I lis-ten and won-der, oh, what do they say?

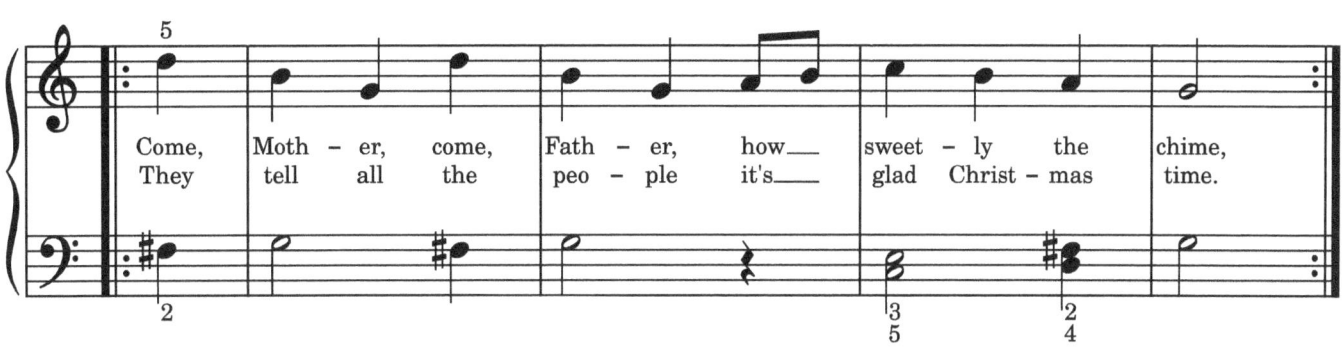

Come, Moth-er, come, Fath-er, how sweet-ly the chime,
They tell all the peo-ple it's glad Christ-mas time.

We wish you a merry Christmas

England, XVI century

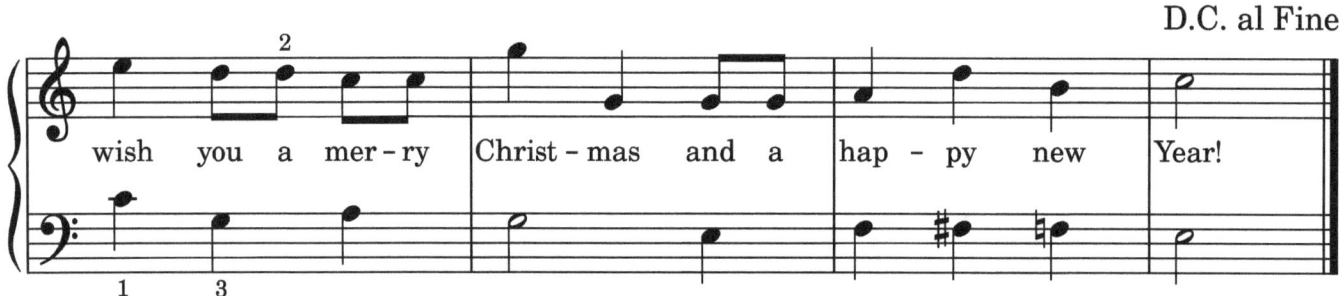

Oh Susanna

(traditional.)

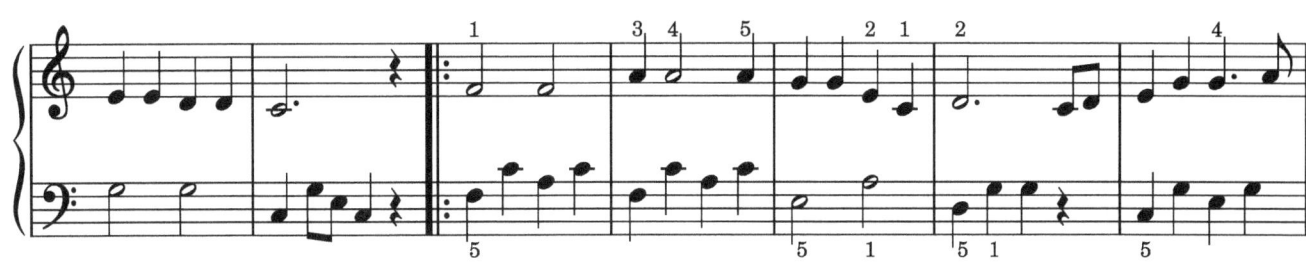

Chiapanecas

Mexican folk song

Deep River

*) poco più mosso = a little faster

A haunted story

unknown author

For He's a Jolly Good Fellow

English folk song

Frankie and Johnnie

Traditional

He's got the whole world in his hands

Hornpipe

unknown composer

D.C. al Fine

Jericho

unknown author

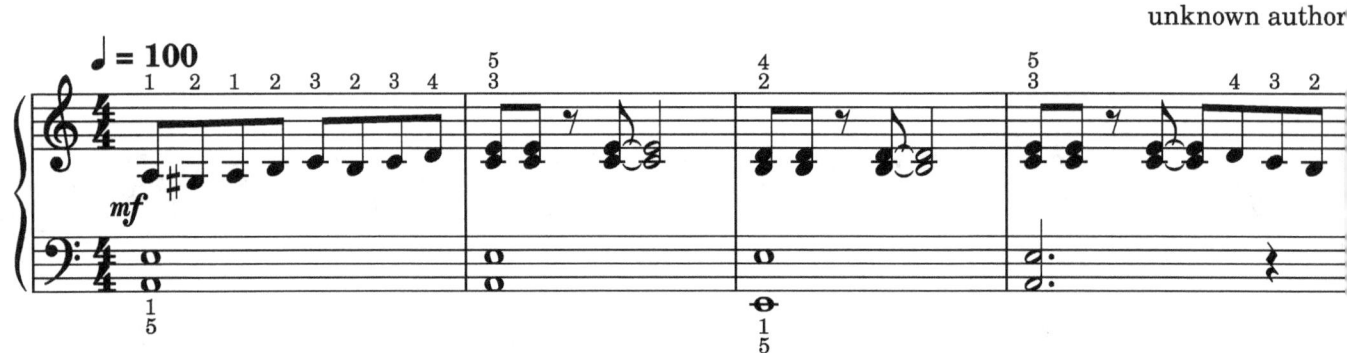
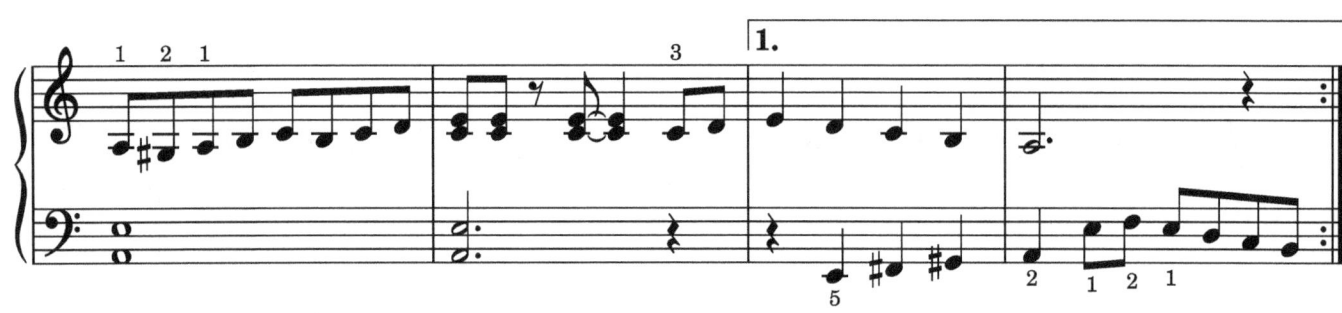
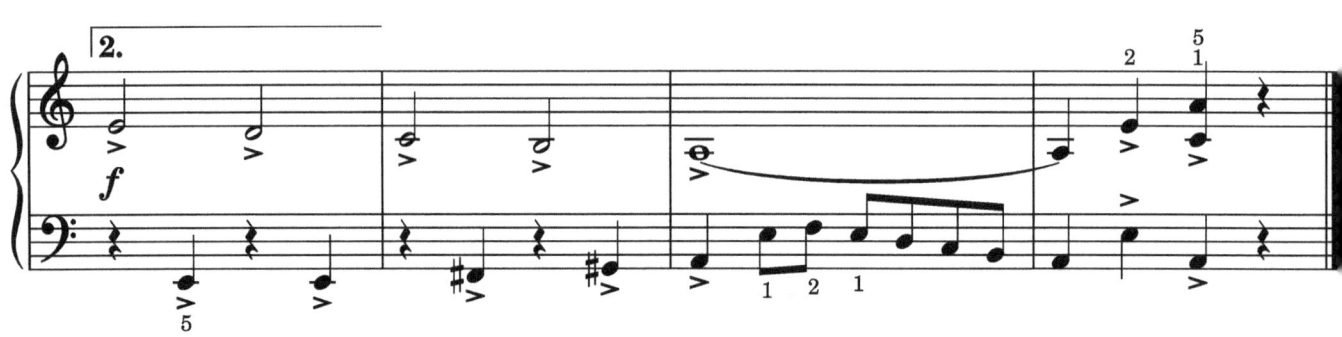

Korobeiniki
(Tetris Theme)

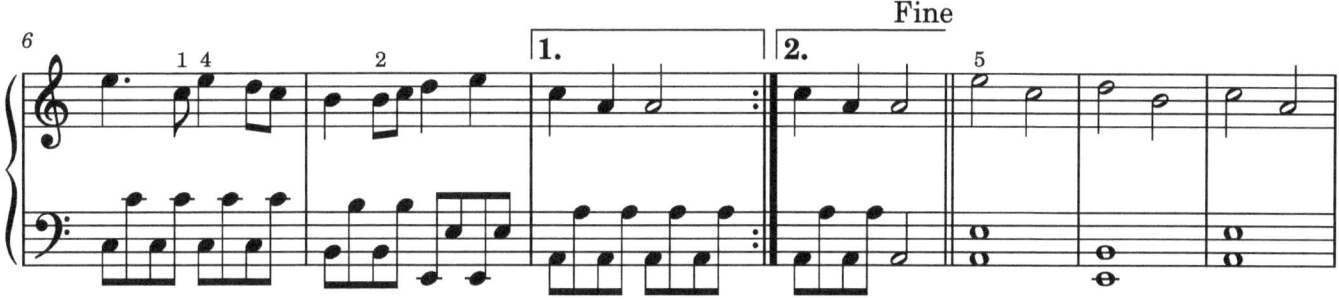
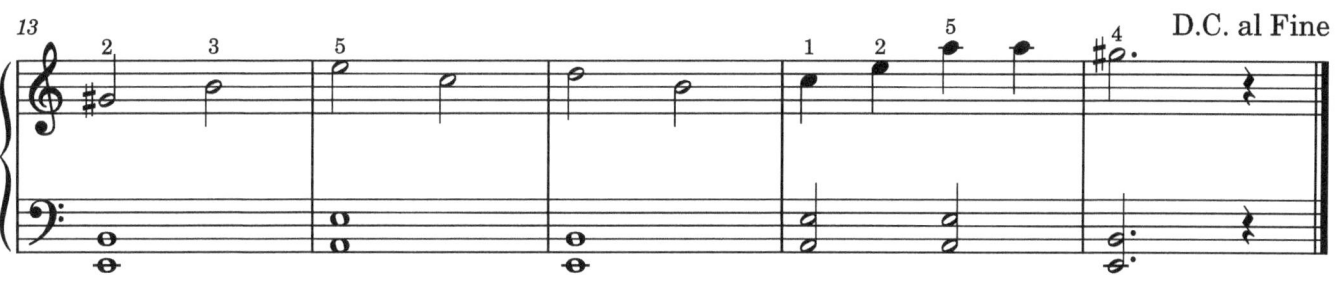

Kum ba yah!

Spiritual

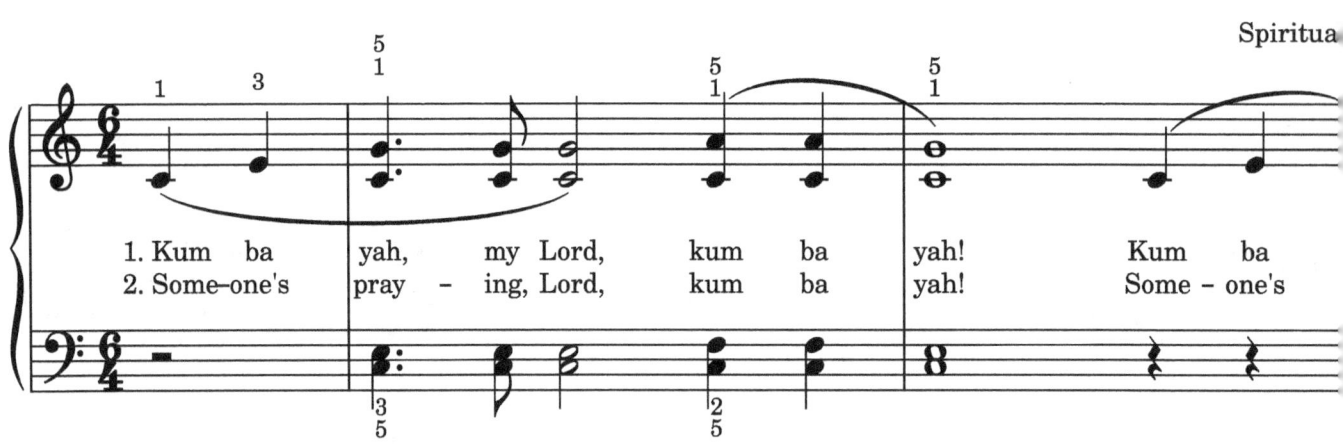
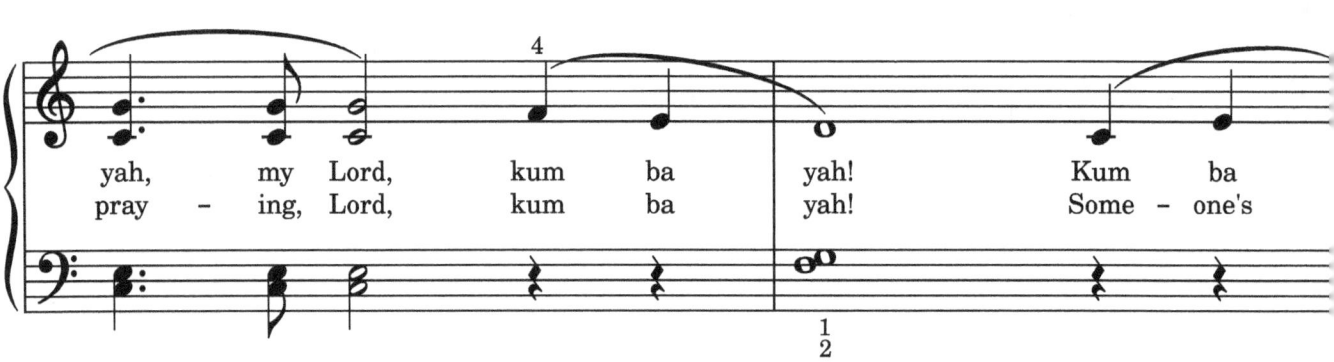
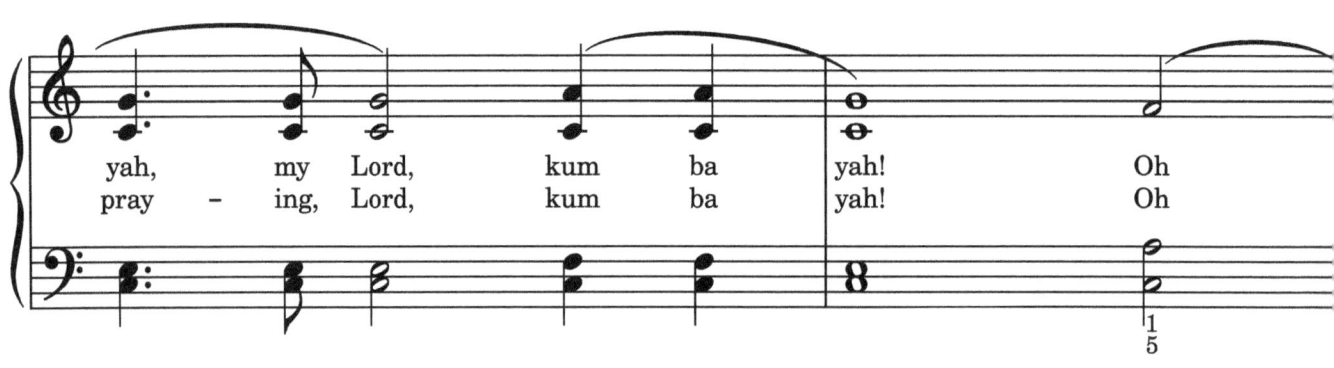
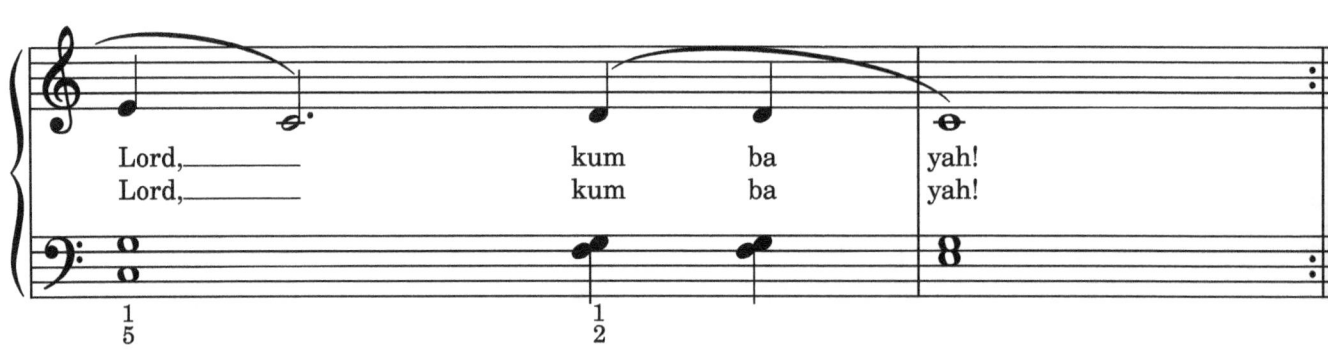

Loch Lomond

Scottish folk song

Andante

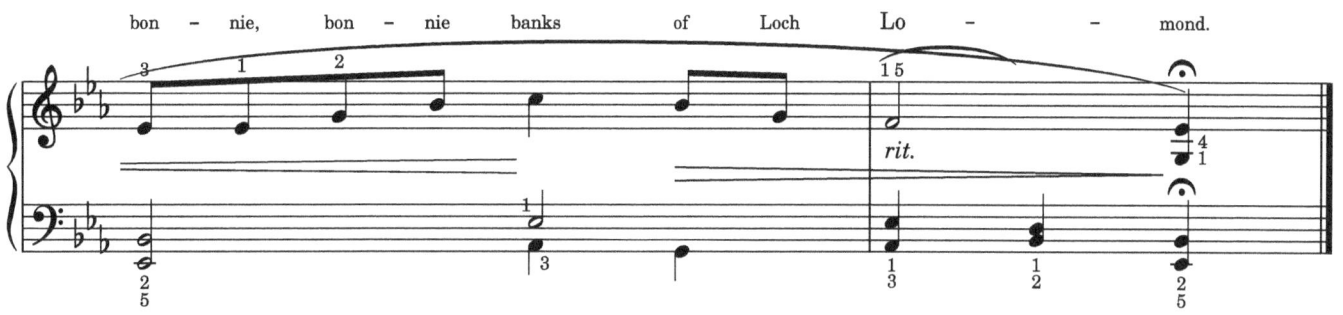

On Top of old Smoky

traditional.

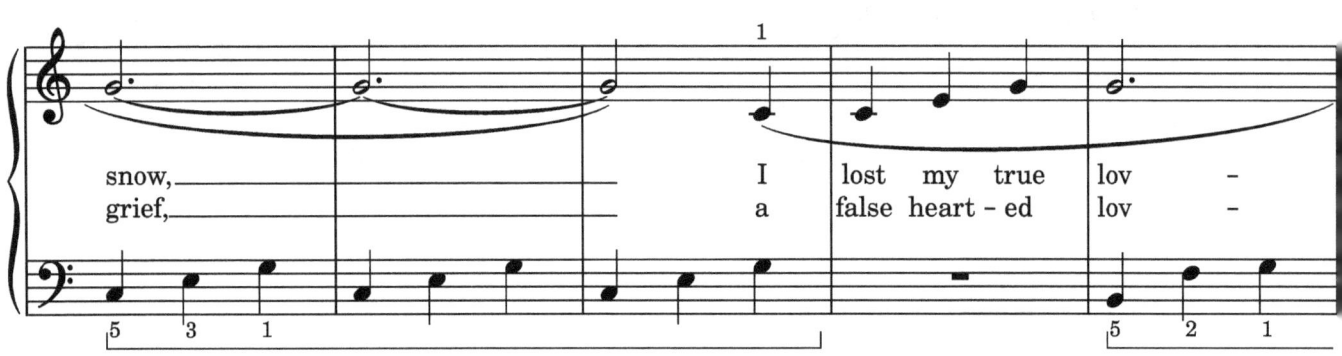
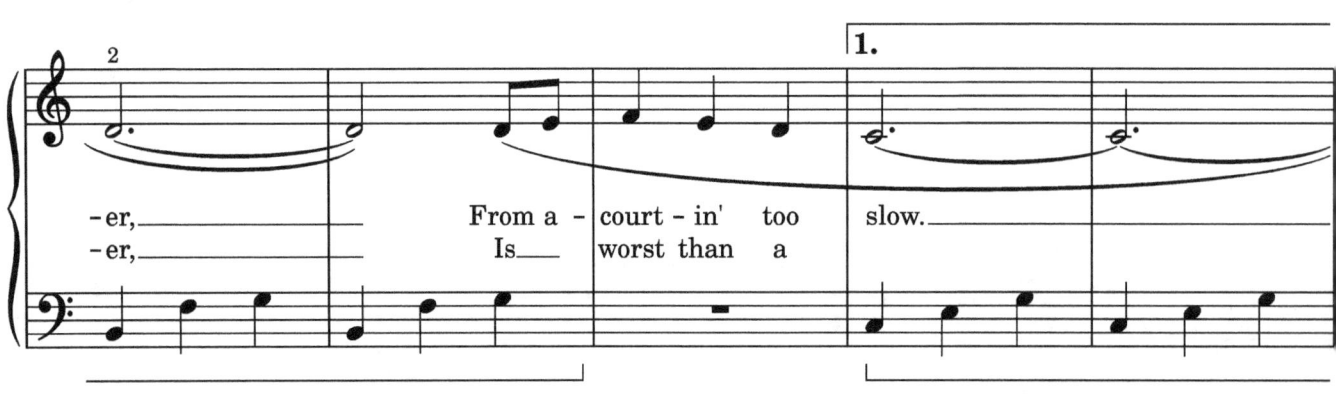
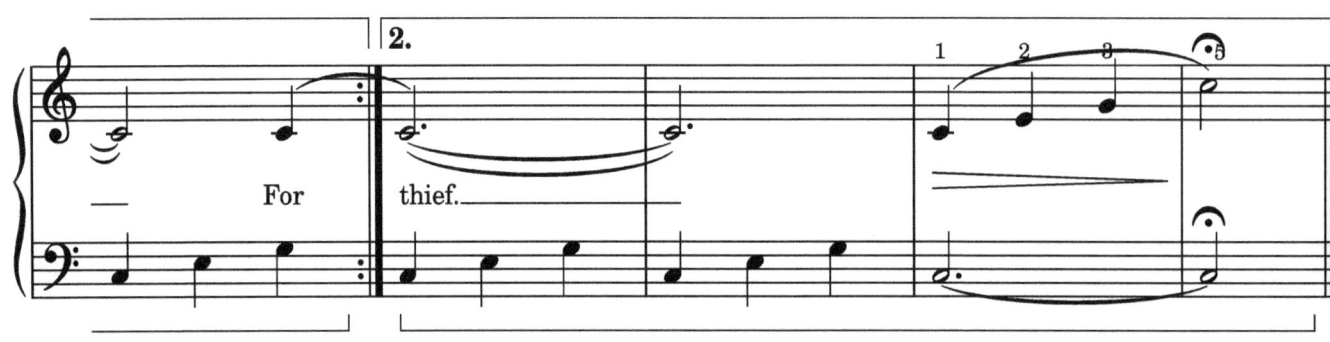

Petrushka

Russian folk song

Roman Holiday

Allegro moderato (unknown composer)

Standing in the Need of Prayer

Spiritual

Moderato

D.C. al Fine

Steal Away

poco pùi mosso = a little faster
molto meno mosso = Significantly less movement

Tumbalalaika

Yiddish Folk Song

Waterloo Hornpipe

from Scotland

Classical music

Part II

Bourlesq
from music book for Wolfgang

Old folk tunes

Menuet

W.A.Mozart

Menuet

Christian Gottlob Neefe *)
1748 - 1798

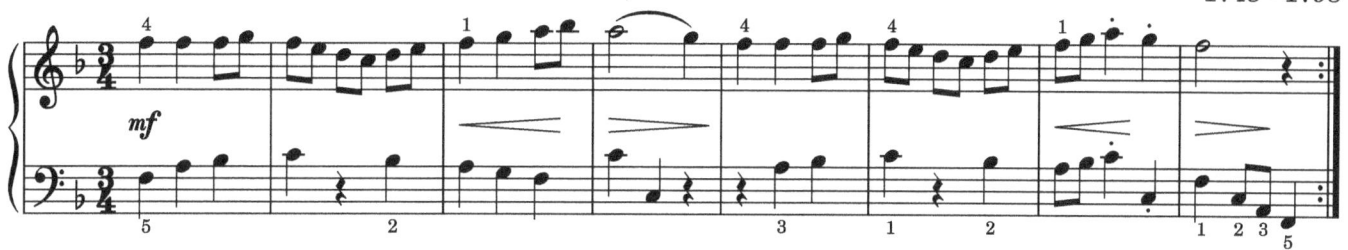

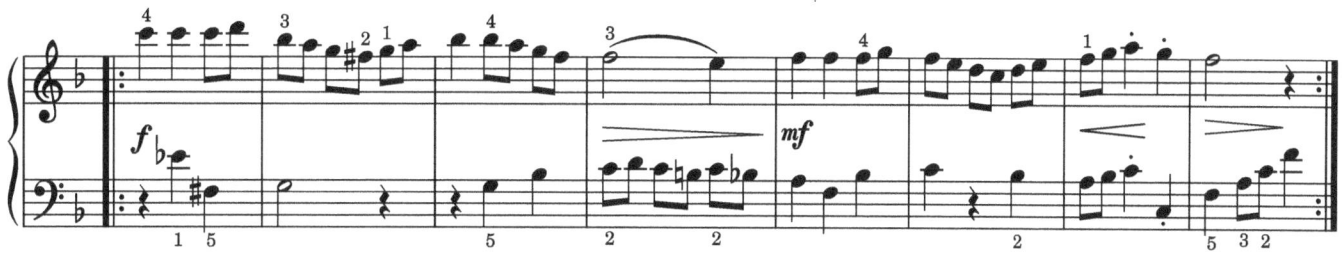

*) Beethoven's first teacher in Bonn

Menuet

Leopold Mozart

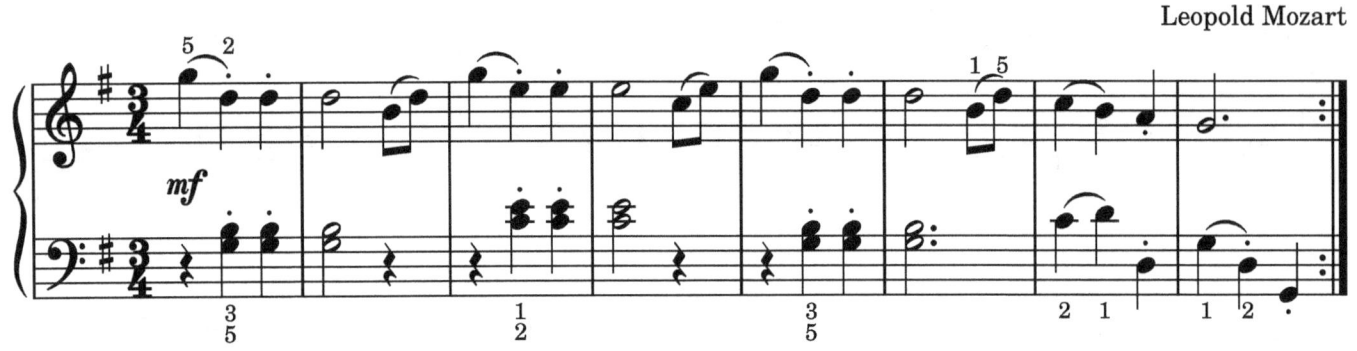

Allemande

Joseph Haydn
(1732 - 1809)

O sole mio

E. di Capua (1865 - 1917)

Swabian Dance
(from: Music Book for Wolfgang)

Leopold Mozart

Joy to the World

G.H Händel

Can-Can

J.Offenbach (1819 - 1880)

Menuet

from the music book of Anna Magdalena Bach

J.S.Bach (1685 - 1750)

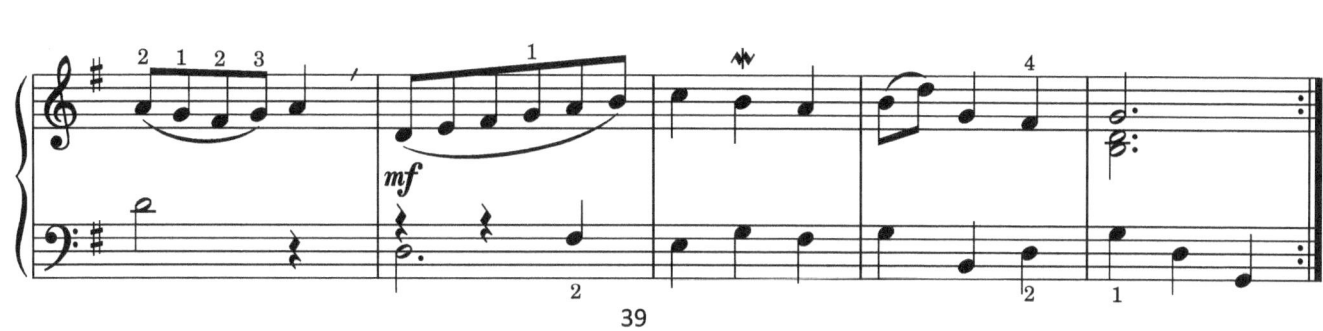

Für Elise

Ludwig van Beethoven
(1770–1827)

La Donna e Mobile
(from the Opera "Rigoletto")

Giuseppe Verdi

Menuet in C
from music book for Wolfgang

Leopold Mozart
(1719-1787)

Shall we gather at the River

Robert Lowry (1826-1899)

Trumpet Tune

Jeremiah Clarke (1674-1707)

Walz in A Moll

B.150

Frédéric Chopin (1847)

Jazz and blues

Part III

Got the Blues

Got those Blues!

Rock it away!

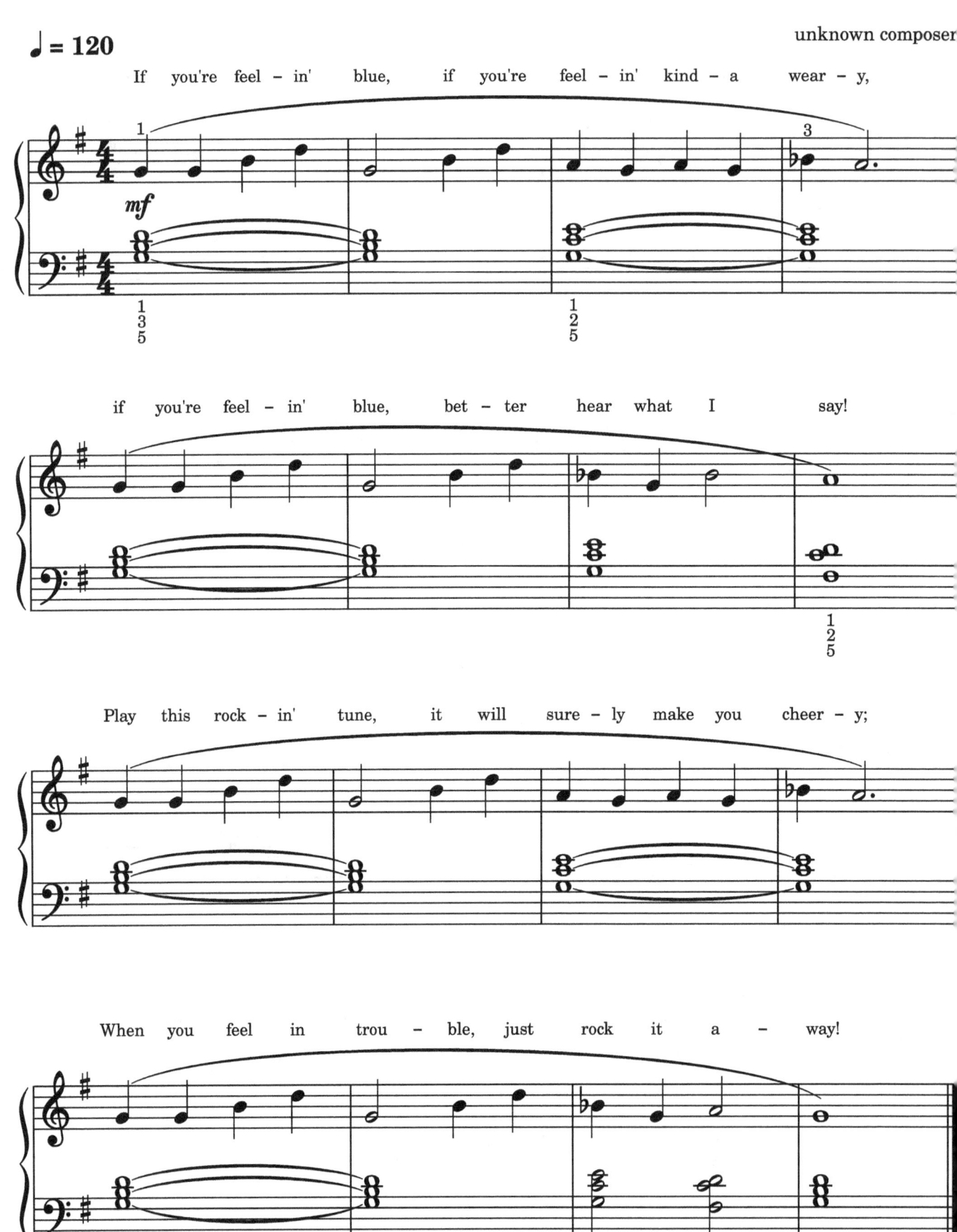

Baby Elephant Walk

written by Henry Mancini

D.C. al Coda

Boogie-Woogie Goose

Willard A. Palmer

Classy Rag

Fascination

Filippo Marchetti (1831 - 1902)

In the Mood
(Glenn Miller)

Music by Joe Garland

Jazz-Ostinato in Cis-Moll

Kiss the Rain

Yiruma

Light and Blue

Willard A. Palmer

Mamma Mia

Over The Rainbow

Music by Harold Arlen

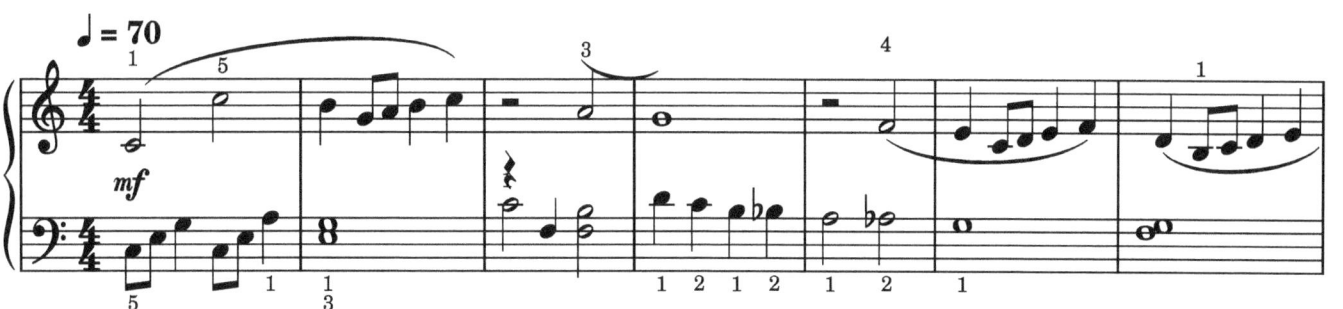

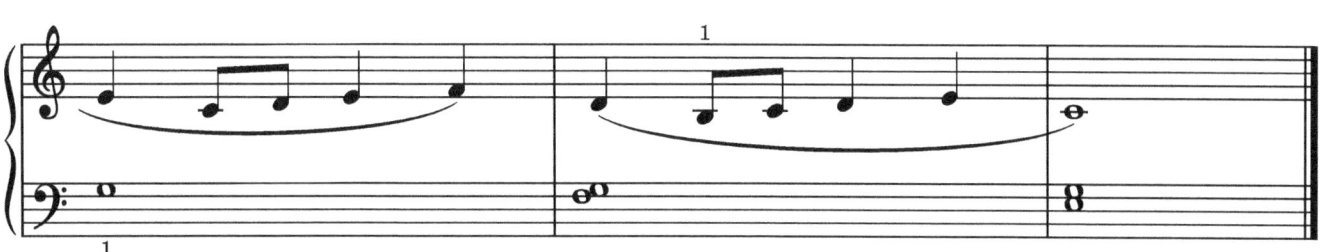

River flows in you

Yiruma

Septakkord-Swing

Sing the Blues

unknown composer

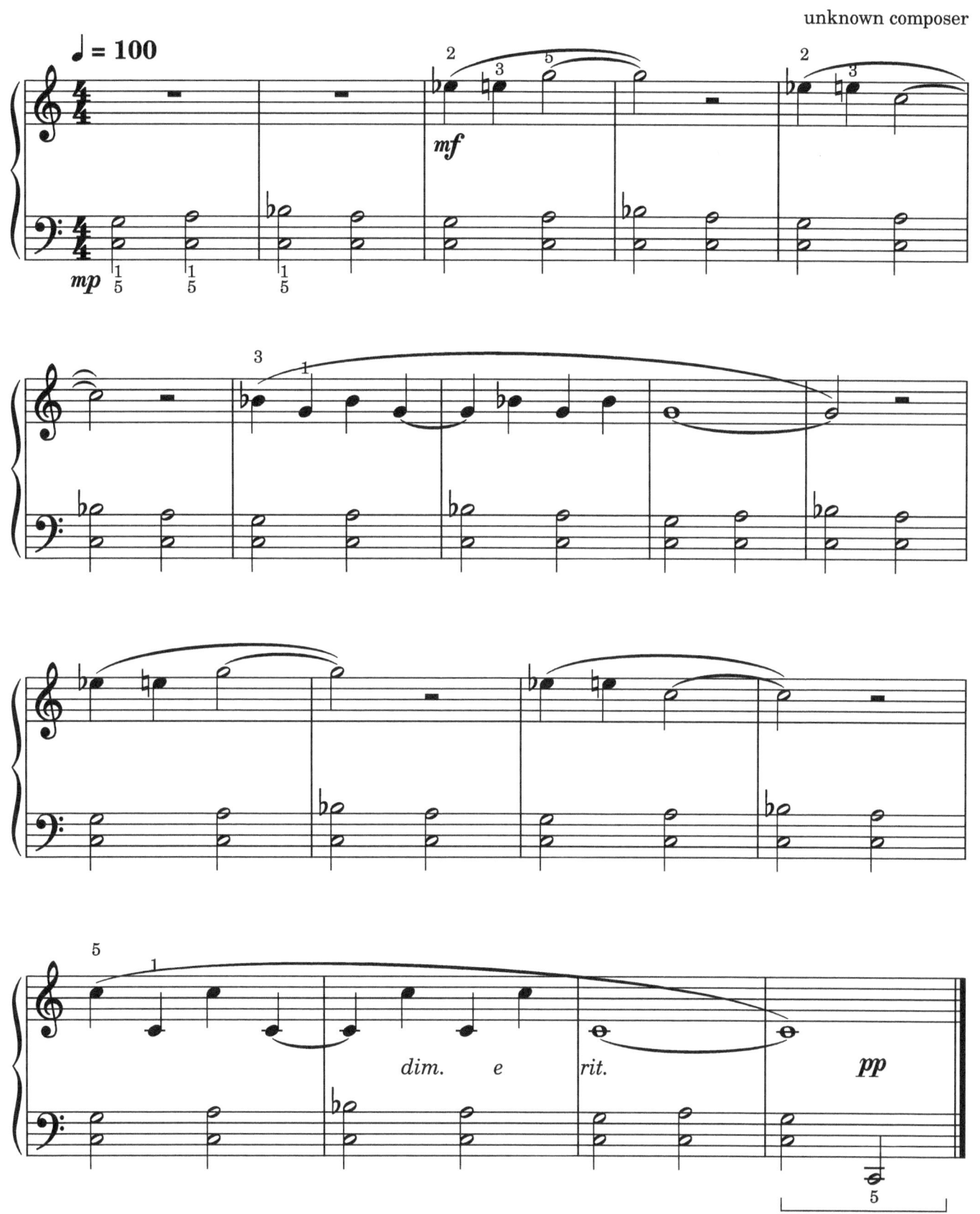

Why am I blue?

Singin' in the Rain

Music: Nacio Herb Brown
Text: Athur Freed

Variations of a Shanty

Willard A. Palmer

Music from films

Part IV

Africa (Toto)

Entry of the Gladiators
(Thunder and Blazes)

Julius Fučík (1872 - 1916)

Forrest Gump - Main Title
(Feather Theme)

Music by Alan Silvestri

Moon River
from the movie "Breakfast At Tiffany"

Musik: Henry Mancini
Text: Johnny Mercer

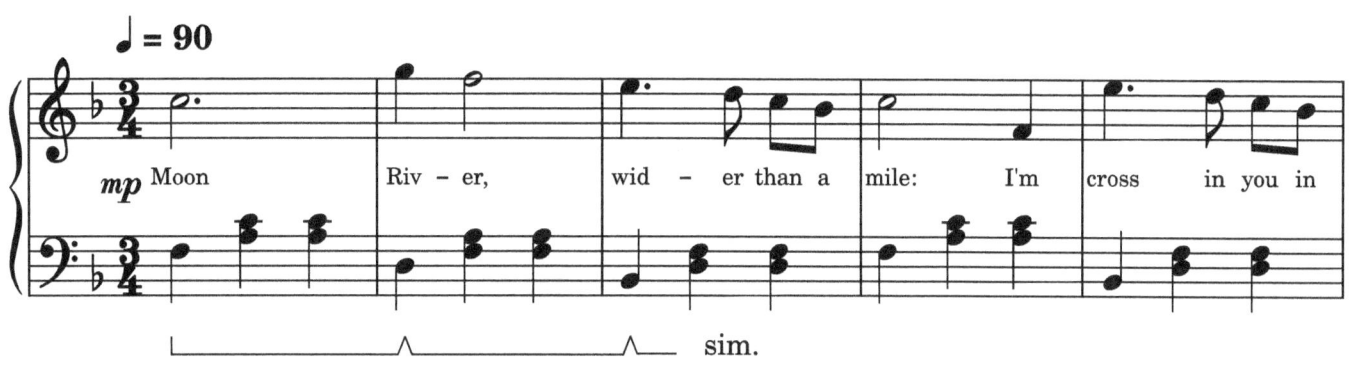

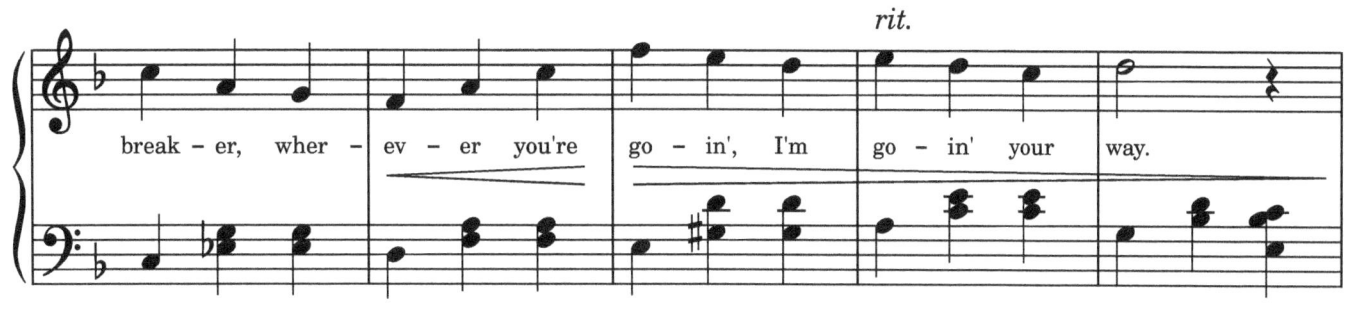

The Pink Panther Theme

Henry Mancini

www.ingramcontent.com/pod-product-compliance
Lightning Source LLC
Chambersburg PA
CBHW080025080526
44585CB00018B/2117